Carrying the Weigh
By Denise

Copyright ©November 2024

All rights reserved. This document is geared toward providing exact and reliable information with regard to the topic and issues covered. The publication is sold with the idea the publisher is not required to render accounting, officially permitted, or otherwise, qualified services. If advice is necessary, legal or professional, a practiced individual in the profession should be ordered. Information provided should not be taken as any professional, legal, medical, or clinical advice therefore use the information with personal discretion.

No part of this publication may be reproduced, duplicated, distributed, or transmitted in any form or by any means, including photocopying, recording, or other electronic or mechanical methods, without the prior written permission of the publisher, except in the case of brief quotations embodied in critical reviews and certain other noncommercial uses permitted by copyright law. Recording of the publication is strictly prohibited and any storage of this document is not allowed unless with written permission from the publisher.
All rights reserved.

The information provided herein is stated to be truthful and consistent, in that any liability in terms of inattention or otherwise, by any usage of abuse of any policies, processes, or directions contained within is the solitary and utter responsibility of the recipient reader. Under no circumstances will any legal responsibility or blame be held against the author and publisher for any reparation, damages, or monetary loss due to the information herein, either directly or indirectly.

Scripture quotations are taken from the NIV The Holy Bible New International Version Unless otherwise noted behind scripture.
Used with permission.
All rights reserved worldwide.

Carrying the Weight of the Senior Leader

Table of Content

Dedication	3
About	4
Preface	5
Chapter 1: Influence	8
Chapter 2: The Process of a Restorer	12
Chapter 3: The Weight of Influence	18
Chapter 4: Attachment to a Leader vs Connection	31
Chapter 5: The Weightiness of Rough Patches	35
Chapter 6: Carrying the Weight of the Leader in Insurrections	43
Chapter 7: Carrying the Water vs Carrying the Weight.	50
Chapter 8: To Honor the Leader Adds Its Own Weight.	64

Published by

Uniquely Me, LLC
Uniquely designed

Carrying the Weight of the Senior Leader
By Denise Bundick-Keller

Dedication

From the depth of my heart, I dedicate this book to my Heavenly Father and my King, who is Jesus Christ the Son of the living God. Thank you for calling me before the foundation of the world to be a voice who speaks your heart to your people, both the redeemed and the unredeemed alike. In your wisdom, you have not only called me to speak on your behalf behind the sacred desk, but to also pen the words you have placed in my heart. I willingly share them so that the world will come to know your heart for themselves. I will love you and serve you forever.

This book is also dedicated to my youngest daughter, Rhena Marie, who listens tirelessly as I read to her parts and segments of what I've written as sentences and ideas come to mind. I appreciate you so much for never complaining and for being my biggest cheerleader.

Thank you to my ministry team and sons and daughters of Dominion Churches International who have stuck with me, held me up in prayer, and have grown because of what the Lord has given me to impart to you. To see you now raising your own sons and daughters overwhelms my heart with the joy of the Lord. I love you all of you deeply and thank you for being the seal of my Apostleship.

Lastly but certainly not least, I dedicate this book to my father in the Lord, David A. Rodgers, Dominion Vision Fellowship International, Chicago, IL. You have embraced me with the pure love of the Lord, encouraging and teaching me to move in greater dimensions. This includes, how to walk out my salvation with fear and trembling. I will forever be grateful to the Lord for sending you into my life. I love being the Lord's daughter, and yours.

Carrying the Weight of the Senior Leader

By Denise Bundick-Keller

The 'One man Band' leadership model has been obsolete for a very long time. In actuality, this model has never been the will of God. Many agree with this statement and say to this antiquated model a resounding, "good riddance!" Leaders welcome the days of working with teams who will help them carry the load. To assist the leader in carrying the weight of ministry is not something the Lord is suggesting but is a mandate given to all kingdom citizens. The principles regarding this are all over the Bible.
Statistics show:

- Around 41% of senior leaders are stressed
- At least 36% are exhausted and burnt out
- Most of the leader's stress is attributed to work-related factors

Leaders who are stressed in their leadership roles not only affect their entire team, which can result in poor communication, poor decision making, misunderstandings and even strife. These issues can run through their ministries like a cancer. To add to the mix, the families belonging to these leaders are complaining that the time spent with them is fading like a vapor. This only adds to the leader's stress.

Carrying the Weight of the Senior leader has wisdom keys and answers on how to not only recognize potential problems and how to focus on solutions to get the teams to properly respond. It will assist in how to help them understand that they have a tremendous responsibility to heavily assist their leader fulfill the mandate the Lord has placed on his or her life.
 Leaders in every part of ministry will find this book to be a powerful tool in helping them convey how crucial it is for team members to carry their own weight, as well as how to relieve the leader from carrying the weight of the vision alone.

Carrying the Weight of the Senior Leader
By Denise Bundick-Keller

Preface:

We are living in a time when to a great degree to be a leader is to be dishonored. The level of respect and appreciation has diminished considerably over the years. The reality is that many are thirsty to be out front and are canvasing for people to follow them by any means necessary. Those who only have this motivation have too often been found to be either immature, unreliable, and/or imposters at best. Due to the lack of discernment, so many people are being deceived by those who know how to move among Christians, having studied them for lengthy periods of time. I must interject here and say, this of course does not apply to every leader in the Body of Christ. Throughout this book, my focus is to reference true **authentic** leaders who are expressly called by the Lord and who have paid the price to lead because of years of their own unique process. They have also been recognized by others in the Body of Christ, who can vouch for them, confirming the fruit of their calling. The price of being processed is a heavy one to say the least. It has taken the leader years of molding, breaking, and shaping until the Lord deems them ready to be sent forth.

Though the disrespect of good leaders is at an all-time high, God the Father has not changed what He requires as far as adhering to the principles of honor according to His Word. He fully expects us to learn them, understand them, and cling to them. Those who don't align themselves to honor those in authority will suffer the consequences. *[Rom.13:1-5]*. I believe that if we knew the value and worth of honor, we would be standing in line to live its principles. One day, we will all be waiting in line at the judgment seat of Christ having to give an account of things we have or have not done, while here on earth. On that day, nothing shall be hidden, and all of our lives will be laid bare. We must not find ourselves ignoring the responsibility we have to honor those whom the Lord has put in place to represent Him. This applies whether it be government representatives or any other sect of society. In the name of what we call "bad" leaders, we tend to dismiss the requirement to honor their authority just the same. Let's not forget David, who honored Saul even though Saul was determined to kill him. David refused to touch the Lord's anointed, even with his mouth. The scriptures teach us that promotion comes from the Lord. He promotes this principle, knowing all the while the intent of the heart and the motives of the one He gives authority to. In the mind of God concerning these leadership types, part of the reason He sets us under them is to sharpen us and purify our hearts. We can never say those whose authority we're under are not due honor.

We must remember that it is the position of their authority that we are required to honor. For it to be "true" honor, it must come from the heart and not just out of duty otherwise, there is no heavenly reward. Being dishonorable may seem trite on this side of the judgment seat but once we're standing there in front of our Creator, it will be too late. Then we realize the importance and value of the honor we should have clung to here on earth.

It is my strong desire to help the Body of Christ examine our perspective on what it costs those who are called and anointed to be leaders. The ones who follow must respond appropriately to them. Both leaders and followers have a price that must be paid to be in order with the principle of honor. Honor is God's design. It has not been originated by man. The Lord will help us understand why those who are called to follow a particular leader experience the things that they do.

Chapter 1
Influence

    I often tell leaders to remember that those who follow them can only relate, to a very small degree, to what it takes to be a spiritual leader. In whatever capacity a spiritual leader is called into, the preparation and process time it took to qualify them by God, cannot be fully understood by the ones who follow. They cannot understand the weight of your preparation until they've come through their process, which will lead them into their leadership call and the price it will cost them. The weight placed on any leader by God, must be experienced for there to be a full understanding of it by others. Specifically, leaders must embrace this fact so that there is less of a chance of being offended by someone else's misunderstanding of why they lead, how they lead, as well as why they do what they do.

    When we talk about the "weight" a leader is called to carry, let's look at what we mean.

A <u>weight</u> is described as:

- The amount a thing weighs.
- A quantity or thing weighing a fixed, and usually a specified amount

- Something heavy: load
- Burden, pressure
- The relative importance or authority afforded something
- Overpowering force.

These words are synonymous with:
- **Significance**: meaning a quality or aspect having **great worth** or significance
- Importance: a value judgment of <u>superior</u> worth or influence of something or someone
- Consequence: generally, implies importance <u>because of probable or possible effects.</u>

    Believe me, I have not taken the time to describe in detail the meaning of weight just to give you an English lesson. We know how much we understand even simple words, but my point here is to clarify, in as much detail as possible, how weight is applied to leaders and the effect their influence has. This is particularly important regarding those leaders who have a true shepherd's heart and whose heart is to lead well as the Lord describes it.

    As I've studied the scriptures regarding the price leaders had to pay; in both the Old and New Testaments, no leader led God's people without paying a heavy price to do so. Each leader I studied not only had great influence over people, whether they were good leaders or bad, but there was always a positive or negative consequence left behind. Also, the good leaders who were able to accomplish great things for Yah, did so while making tremendous sacrifices in their own lives. Yah didn't ask for their permission to be called. Some resisted the Lord's call to no avail. Jonah is a perfect example of this and so is Jeremiah, just to name a couple. The Word of God is true; gifts and callings are irrevocable. *[Rom. 11:29]*. God never repents or changes His mind about whom He chooses nor what He chooses them for. The leader is called to a particular calling whether he accepts it or rejects it. To go through what it takes to be prepared to lead is a journey in and of itself. There is a tremendous breaking of the will before the Lord qualifies him or her to lead. In some accounts in scripture, the Lord eventually reveals why a leader went through a particular process, as in the case of Joseph. Some seem to have just shown up on the scene seemingly already processed. I believe that even if we are not shown the process of some of the great leaders in the Bible, they still experienced great breaking of their will before the Lord placed them in front of the people they were called to. We see this in the life of Apostle Paul as well as others. As we move along in this book, we will look at specific leaders and their unique processes of leadership.

Some of the things I want to bring attention to are listed below. These topics are in no way exhaustive. My sincere prayer is that as you read, the light of the Lord will prick your heart and highlight areas that He wants to personally address with you. I will discuss some of these interchangeably within the chapters. First, let's look briefly at Nehemiah.

Chapter 2
The Process of a Restorer

Nehemiah

Nehemiah rose to the high-ranking palace position of cupbearer to King Artaxerxes, the sixth King of the Medio/Persian Empire. The position placed his life on the line every day. This position gave Nehemiah both authority and high pay. Nehemiah was held in high esteem by King Artaxerxes.

Make no mistake, being a cupbearer was not a meager position. These were officers of high ranking in royal courts. Cupbearers had to be trustworthy on account of the constant fear kings had of being plotted against. Their loyalty was to the king they were assigned to guard and protect. Of course, Nehemiah is the central figure in this book. This book describes his work in the rebuilding of Jerusalem. He was governor of Persian Judea under King Artaxerxes, so we see from just this bit of information that he was a servant, trustworthy, and known to have integrity. It is safe to say that Nehemiah was chosen to be a cupbearer because of these qualities. Not only did King Artaxerxes find him trustworthy, but so did Yah.

According to Nehemiah chapter one, the heart of Nehemiah went out to his people after he had been given a report by Hanini and other men of Judah that the walls of the city had been torn down and its gates burned. He was informed that the people were in great distress and disgraced so therefore, his heart went out to them. Nehemiah felt compelled to act. Here we see his heart for his people, but even more his heart for the Father who wanted to restore the former glory of the city and his chosen ones. Because of his loyalty as a servant, it is important to note that those who have been assigned to a leader must be those who are loyal, having evidence of faithfulness. Not only this, but they must keep in mind that the principal purpose of the divine connection is to help accomplish the vision placed in the leader's heart. Nehemiah had been faithful to the king in his designated duties as cupbearer.

The scripture speaks to us and says, *"And if you have not been faithful in that which is another man's, who shall give you that which is your own?" [Luke 16:12].].* There is a remnant who does not realize that supporting the vision of the leader, allows the Lord to place **them** in the Body properly in the appropriate position to build the vision. This allows their purpose on the earth to also be accomplished. Whenever we are connected to the leader that the Lord has appointed us to, we then discover that the purpose for which we were born will evolve.

Many times, those who follow a particular leader look for opportunities to be close to the leader, but they do not have a faithful heart toward them. They are not sincerely concerned about the vision placed in the heart of the leader by the Lord. Instead, some have hidden agendas which are to promote their own visions pushing them forward out of season. These will detach themselves as soon as they have gained their own following. They become disgruntled due to their own made-up reasons and begin to find unwarranted reasons to disconnect. Along with this, they begin leaking out untruths about the leader to justify disconnecting. What they do not realize is that what they have created for themselves will eventually not be effective. Even worse, they will spiritually and emotionally injure those who connect to them. They will certainly reap what they have sown. Absalom committed this atrocity to his father David. The result was his demise, having been hung to death in a tree by his hair. He did not go unpunished, and neither will those who are of the same spirit.

To imitate those we follow is good, but to seek to undermine their authority over us is not. *"Be imitators of me, just as I also am of Christ." [1 Co 11:1 NASB].* Even though some may not view it this way, this is an anti-Christ spirit in operation. The scriptures reveal the intent and heart of Lucifer, the fallen angel.

"How art thou fallen from heaven, O Lucifer, son of the morning! How art thou cut down to the ground, which didst weaken the nations! "For thou, hast said in thine heart, I will ascend into heaven, I will exalt MY throne above the stars of God: I will sit also upon the mount of the congregation, in the sides of the north." [Isaiah 14:12-13]

This is a serious infraction against the sovereignty of God! We see that the Lord was being proactive to cause a thorn in the flesh of Apostle Paul, lest he be exalted above measure due to the revelations the Lord would open to him. *[2 Co 12:27]*. Therefore, we must be cognizant of our propensity to exalt ourselves over and above both the Lord and the leader, wanting to promote ourselves.

Nehemiah respected his leader enough to first submit his vision to go and restore the walls and the gates of the city. Notice that the scriptures do not mention that Nehemiah heard the voice of the Lord to rebuild the city.
He simply had a heart for his people and then sprang into action. His servant's heart compelled him to take action.
This should also be the heart of each of us who name the name of Christ. This is not to say his desire was not placed there by God. In all likelihood it was, but my point is that we should seek every opportunity to serve. This is a general principle throughout the Word of the God. The Lord will always aid those who have this as a character trait.

All leaders must be careful to never think serving in any capacity is beneath them no matter how many people follow them.

Any who follow a leader from the heart of God must not have concerns as to whether a leader will hold them back from being released in proper time. The Lord will navigate the life of those he wants to release into their own ministries. It is crucial to wait until proper time to launch out on your own. yet. This keeps one safe from premature release, which can damage the one who is in a rush, as well as those who will experience a leader, who is not as mature as he or she thinks they are. A mature leader will allow their mature sons and daughters autonomy to move as the Lord leads them, but it is most beneficial for them to continue to submit to the wisdom and leadership of the one they grew under, even after proper release. Wisdom says, *"Where no counsel is, the people fall, but in the multitude of counsellors there is safety."* [Pro 11:14]. A true covenant heart will be exposed as time unfolds. They will not be easily offended if their leader discerns, they are not readyTo move into the things the Lord has inspired followers to do, as Nehemiah did, this effort must be saturated in prayer before moving towards it. Take note that in Nehemiah 1:11, before Nehemiah went to King Artaxerxes, he prayed earnestly for the king's permission and favor. Also, the King had resources that Nehemiah didn't have.

Nehemiah realized this fact and as we see, when he was asked what he needed, Nehemiah was very specific in his request. Again, he acknowledged that the king had resources that would help him accomplish his assignment. Therefore, it must be acknowledged that even when one has come to full maturity, the leader who raised them has tools, which will greatly enhance the success of the one who has waited patiently for their time to be released.

     Unless followers understand that they do not move in the anointing of the leaders without humbly submitting their own vision under the leader's authority, they will not have all the resources needed to accomplish the will of God effectively. Notice the heart of submission Nehemiah had. He was not one to attempt to be successful without moving in the authority of the King. Because Nehemiah was willing to carry the king's own weight of responsibility, when it was his turn to be elevated with an obligation that would take him away from the king, the Lord trusted him to move in an even greater dimension. Consequently, when Nehemiah was attacked by Sanballat, who taunted him to come down and relinquish his assignment, because of his submission to the King's authority to move, he was able to overcome the onslaught of his critics. In conclusion of these principles, we can affirm that it is through our loyalty to faithfulness, humility, and servanthood to our leader's weight of responsibility, that we are able to carry our own.

Chapter 3
The Weight of Influence

Influence:
• the capacity or power of persons or things to be a compelling force on or produce effects on the actions, behavior, and opinions of others.
• to **sway**, affect and <u>exercise</u> influence on another

Synonyms: imprint, leverage, impact, character, command, importance, consequences, force, control, clout, pressure, leadership, command, and guidance. These are just a few.

    Take a moment to think of a few people who have had an influence on your life. Oftentimes parents are at the top of the list, but in thinking about how your parents have influenced you, think of others also such as teachers, other mentors, famous people, etc. As you think about these, more than likely, we think of those who have had a positive influence on us first. Thinking of them brings wonderful heartfelt memories. We can easily remember phrases they've said that are still imprinted in our minds. Afterwards, we may think of the negative influences as well. These can be reminders of childhood bullies, racist remarks, and other kinds of injustices. Most often, memories of people who have had negative influences on us can be as strong or stronger.

This is because our lower nature wants to hold onto to blame, anger, regret, and unforgiveness. We innately seek to override the inner workings of the Holy Spirit even though we have been redeemed and made alive by His power. Subsequently, the negative influences carry a gravity that engages strong negative emotions. Sometimes, at a very early age, this will distort how we view the world, what we believe we can or cannot do, and can very well annihilate a proper self-imageInfluences have so much to do with how we perceive things, forming what we will deeply believe. For us to be effectively influential, we must have a deep knowledge of how important it is to understand the power of our words and actions.

Herodias – Philips Wife – Matthew 14:1-12
Influenced by One Who Had Legal Authority Over Her

We find that this is one of the most wicked influences we read in scripture. King Philip's stepdaughter Salome, at the prodding of her mother, asked for John the Baptist's head on a tray. We can only wonder how this affected Salmone. What we see here is the influence Herodias had on both her daughter and King Philip. It was because John the Baptist boldly spoke against the marriage of Herod to Herodias, which of course was a sin given the fact that when they began their relationship, they were both married to another.

We never get out unscathed when we're in an adulterous relationship. What begins in lust, and then seeks to be consummated by the Lord, is sin. Herodias became so incensed against the rebuke of John the Baptist, that murder entered her heart. We must be careful how we respond when we are being rebuked and corrected. Even though we may not murder with a knife or a gun, we can most assuredly murder with our tongue if we carry a disdain for correction. Herodias, both a mother and a wife, influenced her daughter Salome and her illegitimate husband Herod, to do one of the vilest of evils; to murder an innocent man simply because he spoke the truth, upholding the righteousness of God. We know this same evil was perpetuated on the Son of God. He was murdered for telling the truth and stood boldly against unrighteousness. Many of us today refuse to uphold truth among those around us for fear of the consequences of men. It is not difficult to be in the presence of those who have a sheer hatred for the truth. But despite the price, John the Baptist gave his life for it. Prophet John did not have a choice in the matter, but his call brought him to his death. Many of us will suffer the same lot if God so allows it. We too must be willing to suffer the price of speaking truth no matter the cost, remembering that *"for me to live is Christ and to die is gain" [Phil 1:21]*. We must strongly consider John's love for speaking the mind of God, whether we are a prophet or not.

John may have never expected to be murdered for this, but consider the fact that John came upon much persecution all his life for boldly speaking what he knew to be the truth. Therefore, in this case, he must have already been determined in his heart to always speak the truth. We too must make up our minds that we are willing to suffer whatever consequences may come when speaking the truth on any level. Many have murdered us with their lips, yet we will live just as John the Baptist is doing now, which is resting in the presence of the Lord in the heavens.

As with Herodias, there are many who have fallen into sin at the influence of another. This covers a wide range of areas, whether it be parent to child, husband to wife, teacher to student, pastor to parishioner, etc. Oftentimes, people get caught up in injurious situations out of a desire to please. Many find themselves too weak to resist, which causes them to do things that they know are wrong. Remember, *"the fear of man brings a snare, but whoso puts his trust in the Lord shall be safe." [Proverbs 29:25]*. Anyone who knowingly influences people for their own advantage will be judged by the Lord. The behaviors of wrong influential people are very easily passed down and are perpetuated repeatedly. These types of diabolical influences have corrupted ministries, marriages, families and governments.

I encourage you to allow the light of the Holy Spirit to shine on any areas where you have either been a perpetrator of this or have purposely influenced others in an ungodly way, being fully aware of their defenselessness against your authority.

God can and will forgive when we come to Him in truth and humility. *"You shall know the Truth and the Truth shall make you free. And who the Son, therefore, shall make you free, ye shall be free indeed."* [John 8:32,36]

Gehazi – Elisha's Protégé – 2 Kings 4
Influenced by his Greed

It is well said that we are our worst enemy. We know Gehazi was the servant to Elisha. This is important to note because we find throughout scripture that much of the training process of leaders, prophets in particular, was rigorous training through serving one already in leadership. This requirement is bitter to some and their resistance to this requirement will eventually bring out the true motive of the heart. Gehazi's responsibility and calling was to serve his leader. To serve a man brings on its own challenges. But when we realize the magnitude of the weight of the senior leader is heaviest, we begin to be honored to assist him or her. It can be very tempting when one sees how leaders move in the Spirit and then aspire to the same thing.

This in and of itself is not the problem, because there is nothing wrong with longing to function under the power of the Spirit of God as your leader does. The problem comes in when there is an ungodly lust for the authority or prestige of the leader without understanding the cost they have paid to lead. An effective leader has gone through many processes before the Lord matures him. The genesis of the process usually begins with working on developing the leader's character. Good character is one of the requirements it takes to rule well. The ungodly workings of the heart will be revealed to the up-and-coming leader repeatedly. Our motives must be purified from self-promotion and from longing for the approval and accolades of men. Depending on how deeply rooted these things are determines which experiences the person will have to go through and how long the process will take. Oftentimes, we think we are free of these character flaws, but the crucible of God will reveal our hearts.

We find that the miracle performed in 2 Kings 4 was regarding the wife of one of the servants of Elisha. The prophet Gehazi was one of the sons of Elisha but is described as "the servant" of Elisha. Initially, the Word doesn't reveal the character of Gehazi, but as we continue to follow the accounts of Gehazi's actions, in the end, his true character is revealed. He was placed in a place of testing which was ordained by the Father.

More than likely Gehazi was to move in the same power and authority as Elisha, being his successor. I believe this is so because Elisha gave Gehazi his staff and instructed him to go to the woman's son and lay his staff on him. The staff denotes authority. Gehazi ran ahead, followed the instruction of his leader and laid Elisha's staff on the child's face. What happened? Nothing. Why didn't the child wake up from his death sleep? It may have been for several reasons. Perhaps Gehazi didn't have faith that the staff would work for him as it did for Elijah. Perhaps Gehazi didn't obey willingly. Or maybe Gehazi was just attached to his leader but not really connected. Could it be that Elisha the mentor, knowing the motive of Gehazi's heart wanted Gehazi to see for himself that he was not ready for the weight of the authority that his leader had? At this point the scriptures don't reveal the reason, but it is wise to keep in mind that Gehazi was in training. I think it's to our advantage to observe this for a second. When the woman came to Elisha distraught and fell at his feet, Gehazi tried to push the woman away. The disciples also did this with Jesus. Jesus had to work compassion in them. What Gehazi's motive is, is what's important. The Father too was working a godly compassion in Gehazi. If Gehazi thought he could do what he saw his leader doing by simply mimicking his leader's actions, he found that it took much more than that. At best he was very insensitive.

We must understand that all these nuances in a follower's heart will #1 hinder the flow of the oil that flows from the leader and #2 the followers' heart will always eventually be revealed. It is important for us to continually examine our heart before God. To observe our own heart outside of the Word of God is deception. *"There is a way that seemeth right unto a man, but the ends thereof are the ways of death." [Pro. 14:12]* The scriptures clearly state that *"the heart is deceitful above all things. Who can know it?" [Jeremiah 17:9].* We must not think we can judge our own hearts. Only the Lord can judge the heart but in principle, the leader is given an inside look at times to judge the actions of those who follow them. Sometimes the fruit of the follower is rotten fruit.

We find, regarding Gehazi, that the influence of his own heart caused him to miss the promotion the Lord already had laid aside for him. His greed for material things was his downfall. Jehovah used Elisha to perform a miracle for Naaman who had leprosy and Elisha refused to take payment. It was obvious that Elisha was not in ministry for the money. The lust of Gehazi's heart caused him to run after Naaman to receive the goods that Elisha refused to take. Not only did he run after Naaman to receive what did not belong to him, he lied to the man of God when he was asked about his whereabouts, not knowing that the Lord had already revealed to Elisha what Gehazi had done.

If he'd only been honest when asked, perhaps his humility may have caused the Lord to grant him mercy. Instead, the result was judgment.

It befits those who serve leaders to understand that the Lord will give the leader, who is responsible for bringing them up in the Lord, a revelation of the walk of those who follow them. Many times, because a leader does not always reveal what they see, one can mistakenly think it is hidden. One must understand that because the leader is responsible for watching over the souls of those under his or her care, they can become open prey to the enemy. Because of the Father's love, He will reveal such things. His core intent is to protect followers from the enemy's ultimate plan. The plan of the devil never changes. It is always *"to kill, steal, and to ultimately destroy". [John 10:10]*. It is best to be honest with the leader when one has had a bout of bad judgment. It is far better to be humble and repent of sin. Perhaps if Gehazi had been honest with his leader, the Lord would have shown mercy but obviously, it was not in Gehazi's heart to do so. Therefore, because Elisha was Gehazi's leader, Elisha used his God-given authority to pronounce judgment. The judgment pronounced affected other generations that would come after Gehazi. Know that our sin can and most often does affect the generations that will come after us. Take a minute and ask the Lord to reveal these things to you.

Then ask Him to uproot from your heart all hidden agendas and to pull each of them up from the root and at the entry way where they began. These things can be so lodged in our hearts that there is no natural ability of our own to be able to detect them. This will involve being willing to see the ugliness in our own hearts. We're all surprised when we realize that what we see in our hearts and what God sees can be eons apart.

Caleb
A Warrior Who Carried the Weight of His Leader
Num. 13:30, 14:24

As we look closely at this scriptural account, we see Moses instructed the Head of each tribe to go into Canaan and see what was there. Isn't it amazing that only one man looked pass the challenges and saw through the eyes of faith the victory the Lord would give the people of God. We see here again that leaders have a crucial responsibility in the Body of Christ. What we say or do not say carries weight. So often the fear and doubt of these Heads of tribes is the mindset of people who labor right beside us. Doubt and fear can be cancerous if not cut off early. We already know that if not detected and treated early this disease will affect the entire body and death is eminent. Many have experienced death to a vision, a dream, or a destiny because of the cancer of doubt and unbelief.

Unless fear is put in check by the leader, the cancer of fear becomes terminal. This is proven by the fact the those who refused to believe died in the desert, never experiencing what was already waiting and prepared for them. The Bible teaches, 'Take heed, brethren, lest there be in any of you an evil heart of unbelief, in departing from the living God. But exhort one another daily, while it is called today; *"lest any of you be hardened through the deceitfulness of sin. For we are made partakers of Christ, if we hold the beginning of our confidence steadfast unto the end."* [Heb. 3:12-14]

I find it very interesting that the doubt and fear of just one person can affect the whole. At the same time, a positive Godly confession will over-rule the doubt of many; particularly when the confession of faith comes by the mouth of God through the leader and not just fleshly words spoken with no conviction in them at all.

As for Moses, it is very interesting to note that even though Moses interceded for heads of the tribes, entreating the Lord to forgive them, the Lord answered Moses' request and forgave them BUT the Lord made a firm declaration that the lack of trust in Him cost them a heavy price. The price was that they would not enter into the promise land. The only one who would receive the possession He promised was Caleb. He declared Caleb to be of another spirit.

We have to understand that it is imperative that we not only trust the Lord when he makes a promise, but we must also trust the leader that He has given us, believing the Lord has instructed them; especially when we've seen evidence of the character of the leader in times past. Remember, it was the Lord who gave Moses the instruction to have these leaders spy out the land. Within the instructions there were specifics. Even after the 40 days of spying out the land, nowhere within that time frame did the leaders start to believe. This amazes me even though they brought back the fruit to prove that the land was indeed flowing with milk and honey just as the Lord and Moses had said.

      Remember this. There will always be the temptation and opportunity to fear and doubt the Lord and the leader. Disobedience will paralyze us causing us to forfeit precious promises. This will also cause the leader grief and unnecessary prayers that wouldn't have otherwise been prayed. There is a deep grief that can almost consume a leader when the instructions of the Lord are not adhered to by those who follow. Notice also that Moses did not select just anyone out of the congregation. The Lord gave instructions to leaders. Here again, we see the heavy responsibility leaders must listen to the instruction themselves and war a good warfare of faith.

Surely things will look the opposite of what the Lord speaks because we cannot attain His wisdom in our finite minds. We must be like Caleb and be of another spirit! In this instance, Caleb took the weight of the leader upon himself. He stood alone with the leader when the other leaders would not.

Chapter 4
Attachment to a Leader vs. Connection

When one is truly connected to a senior leader and not just attached, the protégé must be very aware of the things that come upon a leader regarding their responsibility and the weight they carry. It is crucial for us to understand that there must be a sincere and continual sensitivity to what they deal with. Even more, there must be **much** prayer and intercession going up for that leader. Not many are willing to dedicate & commit themselves to intercede for their leader. Instead, there are many more who will have a lot of negative things to say when they think the leader has made a mistake. And not a huge mistake at that! The slightest disagreement with what the leader has said could cause an avalanche of improper decisions and inaccurate judgements by the followers.

One must keep in mind that the leader, as much as they would like to, cannot share everything that they face. This fact alone can cause some of the followers to be offended. I have made the mistake of sharing too much a few times and it has almost always come back to bite me. An immature follower can easily misjudge a leader's heart on matters, and this will most often cause a conflict of loyalty in the heart of some of those they lead; particularly for the ones who are not as mature as they **think** they are.

Even though it is often said, and is a known fact that no one is perfect, when it comes to those who lead, when there is a difficulty that comes upon that leader, not everyone can handle the leader's openness about it. Most don't realize that this place is a lonely place for the leader. Only the followers who are truly mature can objectively evaluate how to handle what they know. Because leaders understand this, one of the greatest warfares they face is who they can safely open up to. If the leader has a prophetic anointing and calling on their lives, there is a great proclivity for them to isolate, therefore; the feelings of loneliness are intensified. This is a dangerous place because the longer the leader isolates the more Satan has an opportunity to knock the leader off course. One of the weaknesses of the Prophet-Leader overall, is the habit of shutting down and deliberately isolating themselves. Most always, the tendency to do this is rooted in the rejection they've faced over time. This leader must understand how dangerous and injurious this is. With all their might, they must do the opposite. The leader must focus on building relationships with other leaders that walk the same walk and who experience the same type of warfare. To be successful in this, they must be willing to trust the one the Lord sends into their lives. They should pray and ask the Lord to send the one who will give them raw truth about where they are. The enemy thrives on what is kept in the dark. He counts on that leader's silence.

This is a trap. His plan is to consistently harass and weaken the leader in their effectiveness. Prophets must be able to speak the heart of God at any given moment, to any given people, as the Lord speaks. Isolation is the opening the enemy needs to shut down the voice of the Lord to His people. Prophet-Leaders must understand this and again, **fervently** resist the temptation to isolate. This is not easy for prophets because oftentimes this is where they are the most comfortable.

Having said that, the truth is, there are those who will connect to a leader based on something they think they see. I spoke in an earlier chapter about those who have hidden agendas. Sometimes up-and-coming leaders don't realize that their desire is only to emulate what the leader says and does, desiring the result but not the process. They seek a microwave process and do not understand the time it takes for spiritual oil to thicken. What I have said many times is this, one cannot duplicate the anointing. When *'emulation seekers'* attempt to put into motion the things they have seen happen through the lives of processed leaders, they fail miserably. Those who are sensitive to the Spirit of God, will always detect the lack of power in their words and motions. There is simply no witness in their spirit that their actions or words are proceeding out of the mouth of God.

Emulation seekers should take note of what Jesus said to the Pharisee named Nicodemus *"that which is born of the flesh is flesh and that which is born of the Spirit is Spirit"*. [John 3:6].

To the Emulation Seeker, know that by seeking to attach to leaders with a strong anointing but having no genuine commitment, will keep you unstable. Being unstable will prevent you from gaining the attention and notoriety you are seeking. Be warned that if you continue down this pathway, you have willfully missed your own destiny!

Chapter 5
The Weightiness of Rough Patches

There is a plethora of things that a leader will never say. Not so much because they are being secretive, but more so because those that follow them oftentimes cannot handle their truth. Also, mature leaders know how to take situations to the Lord and not to people.

I'm thinking of the many challenges of Moses. There were times when Moses got discouraged by the murmuring and complaining of the Israelites. Every leader will experience this type of discouragement from time to time.

I remember an experience I had some years ago. At the time I was a Pastor, which is long before I was walking into my calling as an apostle. As a young pastor, I began to get discouraged. To me, the members I was pastoring seemed to be moving way too slowly. They were not aligning themselves on parts of the vision the Lord had given me for the ministry. At some point during this time, as I sat in my bedroom alone, I began to pray. I called it prayer, but the Lord saw it more like complaining. I was frustrated. While I "prayed", telling the Lord how slow the members were moving and how they weren't listening, my youngest daughter was in her bedroom taking a nap. While she was sleeping, the Lord gave her a dream.

Not long after I finished having my pity party, she woke up. Within less than an hour, we were sitting together at the kitchen table, and she began to share with me the dream. I don't know if the Lord has ever spanked you and encouraged you at the same time, but He did both to me that day.

In the dream the Lord showed her that I and the Lord were sitting at the same kitchen table where she and I were now sitting. I sat quietly listening, not saying a word. She relayed the dream to me this way. The Lord sat across from me and listened to me while I complained about how frustrated I was with the members. He began to say to me in a mild fatherly tone, "Denise you must eat your food first." I continued to complain, dismissing what the Lord was saying to me just as if He never said it. I continued to whine, and I kept saying repeatedly, "but I want to eat my dessert first!" A few more times, in a fatherly tone the Lord repeated that I must eat my food first. Finally, He quieted me down by saying, "But you **always** eat your food first." As my daughter was giving the details of her dream, I knew exactly what the Lord meant and what he was saying to me. My daughter said she thought the dream was kind of weird and almost didn't share it with me, but I knew the Lord was talking back to me. He was scolding me and encouraging me at the same time. The fact that the Lord responded to my complaining so quickly amazed me.

I knew without a doubt that was answering me through my daughter's dream. He knew I couldn't hear Him through all my complaining. In this one dream, I knew the Lord was teaching me how to be patient and how to wait. As senior leader, I was longing for the members to help me carry the weight of the vision He had given me for the ministry. The encouraging part was when the Lord said, "you **always** eat your food first". The Lord was letting me know he recognized my faithfulness so far. As my daughter continued to convey the dream to me, I spontaneously began to weep. It so blessed my heart that the Lord saw me as faithful even though he was correcting me. He was admonishing me to be patient.

Just the same as my conversation with the Lord was not within the earshot of people, so it was with Moses. Remember the time when both Jehovah and Moses were arguing about who the people belonged to? Neither God nor Moses wanted to own them because they were rebellious and stiff-necked. There are other times when the Lord became so frustrated and angry with the people Himself, that He swore to kill all of them off and raise up an entire new tribe. Still, because of Moses' heart for the people, He interceded for them. Moses reminded God that the other nations who saw God's glory toward His children, they would say the people were destroyed because God wasn't faithful to them.

As we read further, we see that Moses became so frustrated and angry with them that he disobeyed God's orders to **speak** to the rock. But instead, Moses **struck** the rock in anger. This caused God to become grieved with Moses because he allowed his flesh to take over. What Moses didn't understand was that speaking to the rock was a prophetic demonstration of "THEE Rock", Yeshua the Messiah. This is why the consequences of his actions were so severe. The travesty was, after suffering so many tribulations trying to lead the people into the land that was promised to them, he could not enter the promised land himself. Keep in mind that the Lord will not always reveal beforehand the consequences we will suffer for some of our actions when we disobey an instruction.

No leader can allow pride, frustration, anger or emotions to dictate our actions. The sovereignty of God can disqualify us at any moment if we decide to take the preeminence over Him in our leadership just as He did in Moses' case. It didn't matter to God how much Moses had suffered with these hard-headed people. God's decisions are always righteous. Who can instruct Him? He rules and we do not. It is only by His command and instruction that we should move. Frustrations, hurt feelings and even anger will come at times. It is inevitable. But we should pray far in advance before these things arrive and ask the Father to give us great grace to obey Him when they do arise.

I remember a time when one of those that I covered so frustrated me that I almost retorted back with things I should not have said. I specifically remember hearing God call my name and say very strongly, "Denise! Don't you strike that rock!" This brought me back to my senses as I remember the consequence Moses suffered when He took things into his own hands. Thank God, He slapped me back to my senses before the words escaped my mouth.

Imagine how hurt Moses was when those who were set aside by God as Elders and Leaders revolted against him because of envy and jealousy. *[Numbers 19]* They began to lust for the power and authority Moses had. What they didn't truly understand was how much of a personal price Moses paid to lead them, even though they saw for themselves some of the things he went through. He didn't volunteer for the job. He was chosen before He was ever born, just as true called-out leaders are today. Moses went through a deep breaking before he was ready to lead. Unless called to be a leader with a weighty assignment, many cannot begin to relate to the price it costs to walk in the leader's shoes. Oftentimes, leaders make it seem easy because of the anointing on their lives to do what they are called to do. Many times, leaders are misunderstood as well as misrepresented because the Lord reveals His instructions to the leader and not to the populace.

Occasionally, the Lord will have an intercessor pray the need of the leader as He places the specific need in their spirit, but it is the leader the Lord will give the direction to regarding where He wants the ministry to go. At the proper time, a leader will discuss what he or she believes the father is saying regarding the direction the ministry should take. At this point, the Elders who work alongside the leader can and should offer their expertise in certain areas. This is good because any wise leader wants the input of other great minds. This is not the same as telling the leader what direction they should go without first hearing what the Lord is saying to the leader. The wisdom offered is only to assist in being an asset to the vision already shown to the set man or woman of God. Those who seek to intellectualize what the leader does will sometimes begin to find fault with their leader's movement or what appears to be the lack thereof. Some expect the leader to move in a certain way, when in actuality the leader is waiting patiently for instructions from the Lord. One must be completely sure at the outset of who God says their leader is to them because there will come challenging times. At these times, the temptation will be to fall off. Rationalization and not seeing what the leader sees may be because the Lord has hidden it from others, even those who walk closely with him. How many times did those in the Lord's inner circle refute what the Master was saying? What is needed more than anything else is a gathering together under the leader so that what the Lord has in mind will be accomplished. There is no time for striving against the leader and each other. Not only is this necessary, but it is also wise so that those who follow will receive exactly what the Lord intends to release. The enemy always looks for whatever opening he can in order to conquer and divide. To intellectualize is to be part of the problem and not the solution. Even more, we will be perpetuating and enforcing the problem. The leader must be able to depend on the maturity of spiritual sons and daughters to stand firm in integrity through the rough patches and through the things they don't understand. I believe rough patches are not always from the enemy. I believe the Lord not only allows them but orders them. This is important because when the spiritual 'spring season' is about to come, there must be a pruning process so that there is continual growth. If a plant could talk, it would tell us how painful it is to be snipped, cut, and daggered. Parts of the plant that were attached for so long start to get separated because it's hindering the growth of the plant. The parts that remain would probably tell you how much it pained them to see their friends, and the ones who were closest to them, die and then be buried never to be a part of them again.

I know what it is to experience those who say they are with you no matter what, then fall off when something doesn't go their way. There are times when rejection comes to the leader by those who follow, to the point where all the good that the leader has done is forgotten. Those who follow must understand that though a suggestion they made was not adhered to by the leader, it's not necessarily because the idea was a bad idea. More than likely, it was not something that bore witness with the Spirit of God in the leader. We must not forget that God's ways are not our ways. I also know what it is to have one person who is in doubt, and even total unbelief, to spread their doubt amongst the rest of the group. This is a type of cancer which affects the whole. In this experience, it caused a temporary forfeiture of the plan of God. In wisdom, I had to pull back and wait on God's timing to resurrect the project again. The delay was due to having to put out fires where the flames of unbelief took over.

One of the lessons I learned through this is that delay is not denial. Though it took some time for the project to resurrect, I am certain that what we experienced at its resurrection was even greater than it would've been had I moved forward attempting to prove that I heard from the Lord. I interceded and waited on the Lord who honored my patience.

Chapter 6
Carrying the Weight of the Leader in Insurrections

If we search the scriptures, we will find several instances of an insurrection against a leader. One well known occurrence in the Bible can be found in Exodus 32 when Aaron responded to the cry of the crowd who conferenced themselves together against Moses. The people commanded Aaron to make them a god to worship. Aaron, responding to the pressure of the congregation, agreed to throw the true God and Moses to the curb. Aaron came up with an almost laughable idea to create a god. We remember Aaron made a calf made of gold. The people wasted the blessing of their gold on something that brought no benefit or profit to them. They were callous with what the Father blessed them to receive. So, it is in our time that whenever we attempt to force the hand of the leader to act when we think they should, we run the risk of forfeiting what He has already blessed us with. Our rebellion leaves an open door to the enemy to take what belongs to us. Rebellion then gives him legal access to take what does not belong to him. In actuality, he doesn't take it as much as we give it over to him. Wisdom says to search the areas in our lives where we are lacking. Perhaps the enemy has been given legal access to our blessings because of disobedience and rebellion.

Here is another prime example of insurrection against a God-ordained leader. We know there was a revolt in heaven by Satan and the 1/3 of the angels who agreed to rebel against the Lord God Most High. As we can see from the insurrection of Satan, an insurrection against a godly leader is absolutely inspired by Satan himself and a major affront against the Holy God.

The definition of insurrection of course means:

•An act or instance of rising in revolt, rebellion, or resistance against civil authority or an established government.

Without question, the Kingdom of God is the very first established government, and our adversary takes pleasure in corrupting it. I have seen where in good ministries Satan inspired a revolt against the leader. Though not on the same level as the revolt against Moses, I have experienced this. We must understand that a revolt does not have to be on a large scale for it to be a revolt. Revolts are a matter of the heart. Rebellion can be very subtle as well as full out in your face. Through kingdom insurrections, the hearts of the people are revealed. Only the strong survive these experiences. When a leader faces a revolt, it is also a thing where the Lord tries the heart of that leader. How a leader responds to this can make the difference between their success or their failure to survive it; and not only survive it but come out on top of it.

It is times like these that no matter how much good the set man or woman of God has done in the past, very few remember the good. People very quickly forget how the leader prayed for them, supported them, taught them, and laughed and cried with them. Few remember the times the leader helped them carry the weight of their struggles when hard times hit their own lives, and they did not know what to do. They have forgotten the times the senior leader counseled and prayed with them and believed for God's intervention when they couldn't believe for themselves. Here again, we see the power of influence. We can choose to stand and pray for and with the leader or let the dark hearts of others make us dodge bullets. People quite rapidly refuse to identify that leader's fault, if indeed the accusations are true. It will always be amazing to me how people will believe a lie before they believe the truth about someone. Remember when Jesus was accused of being an imposter before he went to the cross? Peter didn't want to be identified with Christ's suffering and denied him all together. He refused to carry the weight of Christ's suffering. But it was Simon, the Cyrene, who helped Jesus carry His cross. May we have the ability of Simon! May we have the heart to help carry the weight of our leaders! It takes a strong heart to stand with someone who is under a heavy burden. The enemy banks on the leader being abandoned when they need support the most.

When this happens, it is only the strength of God and His great grace that can bring the leader successfully to the other side of the challenges they face. Wounds that go this deep take a period of time to be healed, but the Lord will heal, nonetheless. I must remind you that no matter our positions or responsibilities in the kingdom, we are all brothers and sisters who have been adopted into His royal family. *"A friend loveth at all times, and a brother is born for adversity."* [Pro 17:17].

If there is ever a time when a leader needs their followers to help carry weight, it is most definitely in the time of an insurrection. It's in these times, that the opposing forces incite people to become vindictive and downright hateful. People who dislike each other will unite to bring the leader down as in the account in scripture concerning Korah and his company. They came against Moses with a vengeance, and it cost them their lives. Participants with this type of spirit may not lose their natural lives like Korah and his company did, but one can be sure they will pay the price for their rebellion. There must be an understanding that leaders who are truly called by Yah, must be honored simply because they are His anointed. It is always the anointing on the leader that necessitates respect. This does not mean we are required to always agree with them but honoring them must be continual.

It is important for the elders who serve under the set man or woman of God to remember the power of their influence. In some cases, elders who would otherwise be strong, are broken down by the voices of the people they were required to help lead. This brings tremendous pressure on the elders when the people are crying, "stone him, stone him!" In spite of the attack, elders must remain faithful to the leader under the weight of the attack and compel the leader to receive counsel from the eldership he is in covenant with. The objective here is to help him be restored. This is where Aaron missed it in a big way. He decided to appease the people instead of upholding Moses even though he did not understand himself why Moses was away from them for so long. Of course, I am in no way suggesting that anyone upholds the wrong or sin of a leader. But what I am saying is, if a leader has been overtaken in a fault, this is the prime time to seek to restore that leader in the spirit of meekness. [Gal 6:1]. The path to restoration in all likelihood will be a lengthy process, but there must be a genuine motivation to uphold the leader for the duration of time it takes. Again, especially if the fallen leader has truly repented and is willing to follow the counsel of the collective eldership.

In all the years of serving the Lord, it's sad to say, but rarely have I seen this principle practiced to its highest degree.

There are more people throwing stones than there are covering "a multitude of faults." And if there are a few who will stand with the leader in this very painful time, we would see true renewal. To exemplify this depth of love brings glory to the Father.

It was in the uprising of rebellion against Moses, that the anger of both Yah and Moses "waxed hot." There may be only a few, but the Lord has those who will respond to the Lord as the Levites did when Moses asked, "who is on the Lord's side?" At the instruction of Moses, 3000 people died by the sword on that fateful day. We see here that it was the Levites (the priestly tribe) who were courageous enough to carry the weight of the senior leader. They were the tribe that trusted the direction Moses was giving them instead of joining in with the uprising against him. We who are anointed to lead, must stand faithful in this same way when an instruction comes from the Lord, knowing He will vindicate us in His way and in His time.

The consequences of the rebellion of the heart run deep. Imagine how the families of the 3000 people who lost their lives were affected. More damage was done than meets the eye. When we rebel, we should know that the consequences run deeper than we can imagine. For sure the result will affect future generations to come. Legacy can literally be destroyed.

There were times when the Father cut off the entire posterity of a leader who rebelled against Him.

Brothers and sisters, please know and understand that to be a part of an insurrection against a godly leader, is to be met with the judgement of the Lord.

Chapter 7
Carrying the Water vs Carrying the Weight

In this day we are living in there are thousands upon thousands of people who are into keeping fit and so they work out with a vengeance. This is not a bad thing. No, not at all. Staying healthy is one of the best things we can do for ourselves. Our chances of living longer increase significantly. This is not a guarantee of long life, but we will indeed live a better life if we are healthy physically and emotionally. We tend to be able to handle the challenges of life better if we're healthy. Millions and even billions of dollars are spent each year on health and fitness information and tips. We've always known that eating right and exercise is both wise and important. We know also that lifting weights builds muscle when we are consistent.

As it is in the natural, so it is in the spiritual. Our spiritual muscles must be exercised for them to be strong. What builds strong spiritual muscles comes not only through prayer and reading the word, though these are at the top of the list, but also the condition of our inner heart is an extremely important factor as well. After all, how can we purely serve the Lord and his people if our heart condition is weak, if we're holding on to bitterness and anger. Having a poor self-image hurts us too, along with having offenses that we haven't let go of.

These infirmities must be taken care of if our servitude is going to bring glory to the Lord. When it comes to serving a senior leader, it's best to have the leader pray and counsel with you so that these areas are no longer a hinderance to the full purity of your serve. If healing isn't totally complete, one must at least make a conscience effort to hone in on these issues. Being accountable to whomever can help will also make a huge difference. If any of us were perfect, we would never be used by the Lord. As with all of us there must be a continual coming before the Lord concerning this. This ensures a continual flow of Jesus' blood to heal us and to mature us while we still serve with pure intent.

As I previously stated, it takes muscle strength to carry weight. If the weight we're attempting to carry is over our capacity to carry alone, we must admit we need help. I sincerely believe that the weight of the anointing of God and the weight of the assignment he gives a senior leader is so heavy, and very often taxing. He never intended nor ever will intend, for the responsibilities of the leader to be carried alone. We see this principle in multiple places in scripture. In Exodus 18:13-21 this principle is clear.

We see in this account that Jethro, the father-in-law of Moses, has come for a visit and rejoices with Moses in what the Lord has done for him and for the children of Israel, having delivered them from Pharaoh.

He sees Moses has come a long way from where he was when he was tending Jethro's flock on the backside of the desert. There was a tremendous party as Moses, Aaron, and the elders ate and rejoiced before the Lord. The honor Moses had for Jethro is evident. The father-son relationship between Jethro and Moses is hard to miss. As Moses returns the next day to do his ministerial duties, Jethro is there to observe what Moses was doing. I can't help but believe that Jethro's visit was much more than happenstance. I believe his visit was inspired by God.

Moses needed help. He needed the wisdom of God. Jethro admonished Moses to have the elders help him counsel and judge the multitude lest Moses "wear away."

I've been in the Body of Christ long enough to have seen good men and women of God meet an untimely death due to them trying to carry and do almost everything themselves. There were times when leaders have literally fallen out and been hospitalized from exhaustion. Some have had heart attacks and have died. Thankfully the Lord has enlightened the understanding of today's leaders, that teamwork is his plan and not the one-man band. Having acknowledged this, when a leader chooses who will carry some of the weight of their responsibility, it is important to choose those who have a track record of maturity and good character.

Apostle Paul admonished leaders not to choose a novice because of the temptation it is for them to become puffed up with pride and fall into the condemnation of the devil. *[I Tim. 3:6]*. Novices are known to have *"zeal but not according to knowledge." [Romans 10:2]*. This wisdom benefits both the leader and the novice. The immaturity of those we place in position as elders will be a continual frustration to the leader. He or she finds they waste precious time putting out fires and having to bring things back into proper order. Damage control is not something leaders enjoy doing, nor should they.

What is an armor bearer and what are their responsibilities? Is it scriptural to have armor bearers today? In the Old Covenant, the armor bearer was a person responsible for the care of a king, officer or other leader. His job was to refresh, protect, and assist his officer. He was a retainer who carried the arms of armor for the warrior. This was a self-sacrificing assignment. The armor bearer carried the crucial equipment that the warrior needed in order to be protected and prepared for the arrows that would be thrown at him on the front lines of battle. Without this equipment, death was eminent. Take note that even though the armor bearer carried the equipment, it was vital that the warrior be trained in warfare in order for the equipment to be of benefit. Without question, the equipment the armor bearer carried was very heavy, just as all heavy artillery is.

At the same time, it was imperative that the armor bearer knew what weapons were needed and when they were needed. It was imperative that he be skilled as well. If the warrior needed a specific weapon at any point of the battle, the armor bearer had to be alert to hear the instruction and know how to administer the proper weapon at the proper time. Proper timing is important. In battle because of the loudness of the war, it can be difficult to hear instructions because of gunfire and missiles going off. He was required to keep his eyes focused on the warrior and not on the noise around him. If at any time the warrior was distracted from focusing his eyes on the battlefront, it could cost him his life and the lives of others. Consider this visual. It gives us a clear vision of what active and intensive war can be like. Senior leaders are literally on the front lines of spiritual warfare. Therefore, I truly believe that to have an armor bearer who is skilled in assisting the leader is still a necessity today. We see the necessity in the Old Covenant, but we can also see how certain ones in the New Covenant helped to carry the weight of Paul's assignment. In II Timothy 4, Apostle Paul spoke of those who were with him and helped him greatly in ministry. He also mentioned those who had walked with him, but who had eventually abandoned him. Though he was imprisoned, Timothy and others were given instructions on what he needed them to do. This was in a time where Paul knew he was near being persecuted to death. Timothy, a true son as he was described by Paul, was given a specific assignment to bring his parchment. Parchments were made of the skin of sheep, goats, or young cows; therefore, they were very delicate. Apparently, Paul trusted Timothy to bring this very valuable and precious item along with his books. Being a teacher myself, I am very careful who I trust my books with. There were others who were given specific instructions concerning what Paul needed them to do. Being that Paul was at the end of his life, no one could afford to mess up. If you think there was not a sense of added weight to these armor bearers, according to the instructions they were given, you would be sadly mistaken. These armor bearers knew the seriousness of following Paul's instructions to a tee. They knew their leader well and understood how important these things were to him. As I mentioned before, you must know your leader well to serve them in an excellent way. You must study their movements and their habits. Every leader's necessity and requirement are different. What is important to one leader may not be as important to another. You must listen to the instructions, make sure you understand the instructions, and carry the instructions out exactly as they were given to you. If one is not clear on the instruction, there should never be a hesitation to ask for clarity. Imagine how disappointed Apostle Paul would have been if Timothy had forgotten any part of the instruction.

In today's church, the attacks against senior leaders have increased. When a leader has someone close to them who is skilled and dependable, it can make the difference between success and defeat in battle. Not only should the armor bearer be skilled and trained in battle, but they must know their leader well. I cannot emphasize this enough. Not knowing your leader can cause even more warfare. Mature leaders will very carefully pick those who will support and serve closely with them. A leader can be distracted and miss something important themselves if the one who serves gets distracted. This alone will give the enemy an edge and an advantage.

As a spiritual leader who has trained armor bearers, there have been times when the distraction of the armor bearer has frustrated me. When the armor bearer has become distracted by something else, what I needed at that moment almost caused me to lose focus. There have been times when they were insistent on passing me something that I did not need, or on the other hand neglected to pass me something I did. This may seem minuscule, but when you're headlong into releasing what the Father is saying, it's more to it than meets the eye. Once, one of my armor bearers got so distracted while I was trying to get their attention, I felt anger right in the middle of preaching. I quickly shook this off, however, it was an unnecessary distraction that caused a moment of frustration.

The armor bearer must be lion-hearted. At any given time, the leader may give him or her instruction that takes moving in both faith and courage. In *I Samuel 14: 6-17*, Jonathan gave the young man carrying his armor a directive. Jonathan instructed the young man to go with him and break through the garrison of the enemy. As we know, a garrison is a post where military people are stationed. Let's look at verse 6. *"Jonathan said to the young man who carried his armor, "Come, let us go over to the garrison of these uncircumcised. It may be that the Lord will work for us, for nothing can hinder the Lord from saving by many or by few."* And his armor bearer said to him, *"Do all that is in your heart. Do as you wish. Behold, I am with you heart and soul."*

Currently, there is a mindset of some new leaders who think all one needs to be able to do is sing a little, preach a little and even worse; pray just a little; and this prepares them to effectively fight enemies and imps who are lying in wait to deceive. If I could only speak to each one of these types of immature leaders and warn them how big of a mistake it is to have this type of mindset.

I do not call them immature as an insult, but up-and-coming leaders must understand the power of proper process. To allow this, it is essential for effectiveness and even survival.

The plan of the enemy is to destroy their fruitfulness before they get started. We live in a world where people have no desire to know the true and living God, but at the same time are sensitive to spiritual things more than at any other time in history. Many are more able to get a response from the demonic world than the church can manifest the power of God. We need only turn on our television sets to see countless movies and TV shows which depict something regarding the supernatural. The interest of this generation has been piqued to the point where they not only expect to be impacted by the supernatural, but they even chase the spirit of darkness until they get a response. For the church to see and experience the power of Yahweh in demonstration, we must agree with the spiritual laws he has set up once again. We must also be in alignment with, not only his Word but with his character. It is imperative that we are living the lifestyle he commands in His Word. I ask, as did Prophet Amos, *"Can two walk together except they be agreed?"* Those who practice demonic activities have set themselves in total agreement with the things of darkness. Therefore, they get results. As simple as this statement is, many in the Body of Christ miss the importance of living by this truth.

The spirit of a true armor bearer understands that carrying the leader's weight of anointing includes much more than bringing them water and carrying their preaching materials. Though this is a small part of it, to serve the leader requires self-sacrifice. I've heard those who have been trained to be an armor bearer for me say, "People don't understand that we're not able to engage in the service as much as others are, due to the necessity of being engaged in carrying the leader's armor every moment."

What they mean by this is, it takes constant focus and attention to what the leader is doing to protect them from anything the enemy would sneak in to distract them or weaken their time of ministry.

I remember an instance when I traveled out of town with my leader. We were both escorted to the pulpit and after she was seated, I took the seat offered to me which was a seat right next to hers. During the worship part of the service, the Spirit of praise and worship enveloped the atmosphere. As I stayed alert and watched in the spirit and prayed for her, suddenly I saw a man moving swiftly down the middle aisle toward the pulpit. Before I knew it, he was in the pulpit. As I watched him quickly walk up the pulpit steps toward my leader, with a swiftness I was on my feet. Once standing, I stood directly in front of her blocking the man's way and his view of her. To my astonishment, he attempted to dodge me and walk around me to get to her. When he realized I would not move, being perturbed, he asked me to step out of the way saying he just wanted to talk to her. I'm like, really? In the middle of service?

Amid the sound of worship all around me? I kindly stated that I couldn't allow him to do that. At this point, he went back down the steps to his seat. This was years ago, but now we've heard and read news reports of a gunman attacking a pastor right in the sanctuary. Sometimes to carry the weight of armor a leader needs; it will require that you give up your life for theirs. Would you be willing to carry that much weight? Yeshua said, *"Greater love hath no man than this, that a man lay down his life for his friends." [John 15:13].* I am certain that the apostles of the early church would agree that the rewards to lay down our lives for the cause of Christ are marvelous! Because of my training, my movements to protect my leader from, only the Lord knows what, were by instinct. Had I turned my back or had my eyes been closed I shuddered to think what may have happened. I threw myself in harm's way without even thinking about it. How do I know I was throwing myself in harm's way? Just the fact that his approach was way out of order was enough for me to know this was a tactic of the enemy . Even if the man meant no harm, his zealousness hard-pressed him to be out of order. Fact is this man may have done or said something so disturbing to my leader that it could have affected her freedom in the spirit to flow as the Lord wanted her to. It is always about God's people and not anything else. The Lord had a message He wanted delivered and my Leader needed liberty to release it. I stayed alert and in ready mode.

I was willing to carry the weight of the assignment along with her. It made no difference to me whether this man was offended at me or not. My words were seasoned with grace, but they had to be spoken.

As I grew in ministry myself, to the point of now raising and covering my own sons and daughters in the Lord, I have experienced what it's like to be left unguarded and unprotected; particularly while I am preaching or ministering. There were a few times when the armor bearer who was still in training, got distracted or moved too slow to guard me. Each of these times, the people who approached me had a bad spirit. In one of these experiences a woman reached around the others who were standing near me, and touched my face with her open hand, sliding her hand down one side of my face to my chin. . It left such a demonic presence that I could not get home fast enough to take a shower. I drove the hour it took to get home, being extremely uncomfortable with this ugly presence on my face. I rushed to get into the shower and scrubbed my face for the longest time, but the residue which was left on me would not come off with a mere shower. Whatever that spirit was would not leave me until I continued for a while in prayer. Eventually that spirit had no choice but to leave. I have had a few other of these types of experiences, but I only wanted to give you a peek into to my life as both an armor bearer and as a leader.

The necessity for covering your leader is real and important. Leaders are in war while they move forward in their God given assignments. The enemy will do anything he can to cause confusion and distraction while the Lord is speaking to His people. Preaching is not just preaching. Preaching throws a leader right on the front lines of battle. *"How can they hear without a preacher and how shall he preach except he be sent?"* [Rom 10:14-15]. When a preacher is sent into battle with a message, it is imperative that the Word of God be delivered. As far as the characteristics of a true armor bearer goes, let's look.

The responsibilities and duties of an armor bearer must be clearly understood so that he or she is a tremendous help to the leader. To be alert is imperative, and to serve with a pure heart and spirit is just as crucial. I have had the unpleasant experience of putting out fires between armor bearers, who were in competition with each other. I've also had the remarkable benefit of being served by two armor bearers who were serving me at the same time. They worked together like a well-oiled machine, and I benefitted greatly as they served. Those who serve in this capacity should go before the Lord in prayer ahead of time in order to cleanse their own hearts and to ask the Lord for His help so that their service is at its optimum capacity. The enemy loves to initiate war games and war games are certainly not a game! Having said this, I never take those who serve me for granted.

They are not peons. They are servants of the Lord and should be handled as such. It can be easy to forget this but remember not to forget the word which teaches us, *"But he that is greatest among you shall be your servant."* [Matt 23:11]

Other responsibilities of the armor bearer are lived out after the ministry assignment is over. A heart of submission to the leader is continual; so is respect, as well as keeping alert while the leader rests for a while after coming off the battlefield of ministry. Most times, the leader does not share regarding the psychological attack they war against afterward. The devil hates the effectiveness of the anointed word that changes the lives of people. Therefore, he is determined to make the leader pay for it. Armor bearers must be intolerant of accusations, rumors, or gossip about the leader overall but even more so after the preached word. The enemy is expert at creating holes where he can slip in, and cause hurt or confusion among the people around him. Some look at armor bearers with envy but all they can see is that they walk closely with the leader. They do not see that the armor bearer as well as the leader are in constant spiritual warfare.

As you can see, there is a sharp contrast between carrying the leader's weight and just carrying the leader's water.

Chapter 8
To Honor the Leader Adds Its Own Weight

"Obey your leaders and submit to them, for they are keeping watch over your souls, as those who will have to give an account. Let them do this with joy and not with groaning, for that would be of no advantage to you." [Hebrews 13:17]. When a leader truly buys into the truth and importance of these words, many leaders will sweat in gut-wrenching prayer until things are properly aligned.

The command in scripture is this, *"Let love be genuine. Abhor what is evil; hold fast to what is good. Love one another with brotherly affection. Outdo one another* **in showing honor**. *Do not be slothful in zeal, be fervent in spirit, serve the Lord. Rejoice in hope, be patient in tribulation, be constant in prayer. Contribute to the needs of the saints and seek to show hospitality." [Romans 12:9-13* ESV] Unless one's spirit is broken, this is difficult to do; depending on the natural disposition. It's a tall order for many but still, it is not a suggestion by the Apostle Paul.

Honoring your leader is a form of honoring all authority. One cannot think they are in order by honoring their spiritual leaders but dishonoring those in authority everywhere else. To honor is a principle that does not end in the church. When we set our hearts to honor our leaders, it is by this heart attitude, and demonstration, that we truly honor the Lord. The commandment to honor comes from Him. He did not suggest it, He commanded it. When it comes to our parents, keep in mind that it is one of the ten commandments.We know it is the first commandment that has a promise attached to it, which is *"that thy days may be long upon the land."* [Ex. 20:12].

1 Timothy 5:17 speaks of giving leaders who **rule** well double or two-fold honor; especially those who labor in the word and doctrine. The Greek word for labor in this scripture is the same meaning as the word toil. To **toil** means: 'to engage in hard and continuous work; to move or travel with difficulty, weariness or pain'.

To understand the context of this word according to the language it was written in, we have a clearer picture of what a good leader experiences in order to get a true, clear, and concise message to God's people.

Good leaders make what they do seem easy because of the anointing that is on them to execute the mind and will of God. As we see here, this is not as easy as it looks. The Lord fully intends to apply weight to those who follow leaders, commanding that they honor. Most have stopped at verse 17 but have not properly connected verse 18 to it, which reads "for the scripture saith thou shalt not muzzle the ox that treadeth out the corn, and the laborer is worthy of his reward." The reward of the laborer is also not a suggestion, but it is without a doubt an instruction that should be obeyed. Paul referred to the word of God that has already been written, so we see this instruction was not by Paul's own command. Even if it had been, because all scripture is by "inspiration of the Spirit", the instruction would still have been correct. Oftentimes, people forget that their obedience is not only noted by God, but it has opened the door to blessings. All obedience to Him, one way or another, brings blessing and reward; therefore, it is a requirement to obey biblical instruction no matter what the instruction is. *Proverbs 3:9* states, *"honor the Lord with thy substance and with the first fruits of all thine increase."* Be assured dear reader, that by releasing your substance it goes into your heavenly account which will bring great reward. By not adhering to this instruction, we may not realize that this places us right in the category of trying to serve God and mammon at the same time. To serve the two simultaneously is impossible. Whether we can embrace this truth or not, it is nonetheless the truth. We will love one and hold to it and despise whichever one we do not choose. If we choose unrighteous mammon, then we have despised the way of the Lord. The Lord used Matthew to pen this instruction once and used Luke to pen it also. Luke went another step further and wrote, *"if therefore ye have not been faithful in the unrighteous mammon, who will commit to your trust the true riches?"* Certainly, it is not the Lord who will trust us. Our track record proves to Him that we cannot be trusted.

To respect and to honor are synonymous. However, to honor adds to a higher level. To honor someone means to do what is required or desired. To stand and testify saying, "I honor my leader" is not the depth of true honor. For some, to say this, these words are only mere words. But when the action of doing what is required or desired by the leader, this is what indicates true honor from the heart. We can say all day that we "honor" the Lord, but not do a thing that He desires or requires. To truly honor, there must be an action attached to the words. In *Malachi 1:6* the Lord asks, *"where is my honor?"* He lays it on the line saying, *"if a son honors his father, and a servant honors his master, if you say I am your Father then where is MY honor?'* In this account, the Lord is chastising the priests for offering unto Him bread that was polluted with the lack of obedience to how it was to be served.

Honor should only be given to those who are worthy of it. We can show respect to anyone, but honor goes to those who have shown they deserve it. It is virtually impossible to really honor someone until you can recognize who and what they are.

When someone who is deserving of honor receives it, they will always return honor back to the one who has honored them.

Lastly, we must understand that honor can also be lost. How? There are several ways this happens. Honor can be lost when you join yourself to dishonorable people. It can also be lost when you dishonor the Lord's appointed representatives. Be careful not to yield to the temptation to sin being seduced by the dictates of your flesh or the devil. You run the risk of losing honor. The adversary would love nothing more than to laugh you to scorn because you yielded to the dictates of these two enemies. Also, doing the right thing for the wrong reason or with the wrong motive will thrust you into the place of dishonor. Another way, which is extremely important, is to try to establish yourself in a position that the Lord has not given you. He will without a doubt remove you from a position that he has not appointed. Another way honor is produced is by defending those in authority. In this case, even though people may not always honor you, the Lord will. This is the place to decide who you really want to please and honor. We never lose our reward by fully obeying Him. Therefore, as you consider the weight that honor holds in your life, pursue the strength of the Lord to carry it. Rewards given out in heaven will be more than amazing.

Made in the USA
Columbia, SC
05 December 2024